Autobiographies You Never
Thought You'd Read

BIGFOOT

Catherine Chambers

heinemann
raintree

© 2016 Heinemann-Raintree
an imprint of Capstone Global Library, LLC
Chicago, Illinois

To contact Capstone Global Library please call 800-747-4992, or visit our web site www.capstonepub.com

Edited by Linda Staniford
Designed by Steve Mead
Original illustrations © Capstone Global Library Ltd 2015
Illustrated by Ryan Petney - Advocate Art
Production by Victoria Fitzgerald
Originated by Capstone Global Library Ltd
Printed and bound in China by Leo Paper Products

19 18 17 16 15
10 9 8 7 6 5 4 3 2 1

Library of Congress Cataloging-in-Publication Data
Chambers, Catherine, 1954-
  Bigfoot / Catherine Chambers.
      pages cm.—(Autobiographies you never thought you'd read)
  Includes bibliographical references and index.
  ISBN 978-1-4109-7961-2 (hb)—ISBN 978-1-4109-7966-7 (pb)—ISBN 978-1-4109-7976-6 (ebook) 1. Sasquatch—Juvenile literature. I. Title.
  QL89.2.S2C43 2015
  001.944—dc23   2015000251

Acknowledgments
Every effort has been made to contact copyright holders of material reproduced in this book. Any omissions will be rectified in subsequent printings if notice is given to the publisher.

All the Internet addresses (URLs) given in this book were valid at the time of going to press. However, due to the dynamic nature of the Internet, some addresses may have changed, or sites may have changed or ceased to exist since publication. While the author and publisher regret any inconvenience this may cause readers, no responsibility for any such changes can be accepted by either the author or the publisher.

Contents *

Some words are shown in bold, **like this**. You can find out what they mean by looking in the glossary.

Who Am I?
Where Am I From?

I am Bigfoot. Some people call me Sasquatch. I come from North America. This map shows where people have reported seeing me in the United States and Canada.

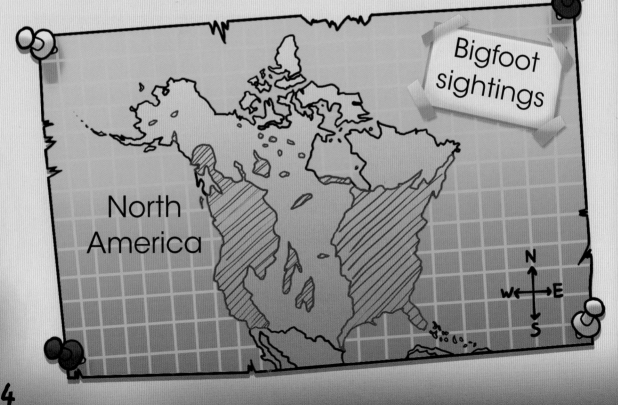

Bigfoot sightings

North America

N
W E
S

Some **American Indians** on the East Coast talk of a creature called Windigo. Others speak of Ha'yacatsi. It means "Lost Giant," because he's huge and likes to hide. But are they the same as me?

DID YOU KNOW?

The name Sasquatch was created from American Indian names such as Sokqueatl and Soss-q'tal.

What Do I Look and Smell Like?

Some people say I am very tall and hairy. Others say I look like a ghost or a stone giant.

But the Chickasaw people of the Southeastern woodlands talk of Lofa, a smelly, hairy beast. Now that's not very nice! Surely that's not me?

DID YOU KNOW?

Hunters say that Bigfoot leaves a lingering bad smell wherever it goes.

Do I Live Alone?

Some people think I am on my own all the time, but I have a sister. She's smaller than me and less hairy. People who have seen her say she's cleaner, too. Hmmm, I have no idea what they mean...

DID YOU KNOW?

The Kwakiutl and Tlingit peoples of Northwest Canada tell tales of Tsunoqua. She's a big, wild woman who lives in the woods.

How Old Am I?

It's hard to tell my age. But as I get older, I start to stoop. My hair turns gray and dangles off my body. Well, that's what humans say. **American Indians** have been telling tales about me and my family for years.

DID YOU KNOW?

Hunters say they have seen Bigfoot with black or red-brown hair.

How Do I Move?

My legs are long but never straight. I move smoothly on my two legs, using long strides. Some say I can run as fast as a horse!

DID YOU KNOW?

An adult Bigfoot footprint is said to be about 15 inches (38 centimeters) long. Its stride can reach 5 feet (1.5 meters).

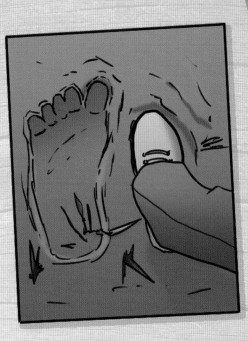

Where Do I Live?

I live mostly in thick woodland. Humans say they have found my food waste in caves, too. But I'm keeping the location of my home a secret.

I like to wander near rivers and lakes.
You might even see me enjoying a swim.

What Do I Eat?

My parents taught me how to find nuts and berries. Some humans say I kill deer or even pet dogs and cats.

The Comanche people of the Southern Plains tell tales of Mu Pitz, a **cannibal** monster. Is that really me? I don't think so.

DID YOU KNOW?

Some hunters say they have found stashes of corn stolen by Bigfoot.

Do I Hibernate?

Some humans think I store food for winter **hibernation**. It's certainly hard to hunt and gather in dark, chilly months. So I store fat in a hump on my back to help me through.

But I don't hibernate. You might find my footprints in the snow! I hide and watch hunters tracking them!

Am I Fierce?

I think I'm a really nice guy. But some people say we like to throw rocks. And some even claim that Tsunoqua, the wild woman, roasts children and eats them! Terrible tales like this might scare you away from folks like us!

DID YOU KNOW?

Some people say that European **lumberjacks** heard old tales like Tsunoqua's around the campfire. Did these people make up Bigfoot based on what they'd heard?

Am I a Ghost?

The Kwakiutl people of Vancouver Island, Canada, believe in a big ghostly creature. They call him Bukwus, which means "the wild Ghost Chief from the woods." According to these people, Bukwus likes to offer humans some of his food. Then he turns them into a Bukwus, too! Could Bukwus be me?

DID YOU KNOW?

Kwakiutl artists carve colorful Bukwus masks. They are worn during ceremonies and **solemn** dances.

Are These Tales Real?

Are these real tales or tall tales? My grandma says that 100 years ago, there was a teacher named J. W. Burns. He collected stories about wild men, whom he named Sasquatch.

DID YOU KNOW?

Many clubs today organize Bigfoot hunts. They use cameras and electrical equipment to look for him.

Have You Spotted Me?

You think you've spotted me, but have you really? Some of you say you've found my footprints and my knuckle prints. Some even say they found my poo! Is it true? Or am I just smarter than you?

DID YOU KNOW?

There have been many fake Bigfoot finds, from bears' fur to footprints made with plaster models!

Do I Really Exist?

Of course, I believe I exist. I even have family in other parts of the world. My **Yeti** cousins live in the **Himalayan** mountain range. Others live in Africa.

You can tell we are related. We are all big, hairy, and very shy. I hope humans will never harm us.

DID YOU KNOW?

Some say that Bigfoot is descended from an ancient great ape called Gigantopithecus.

Glossary

American Indian first people who arrived in North America thousands of years ago

cannibal creature that eats other creatures of its own kind

hibernation when the body slows down a lot in winter. Some creatures sleep through the winter.

Himalaya mountain range in Asia

lumberjack someone who cuts down trees

solemn very serious

Yeti huge, hairy creature like a Bigfoot, but found in the Himalayan mountains

Find Out More

You could find out more about Bigfoot and Bigfoot hunters in other books and on the Internet.

Books

Burgan, Michael. *The Unsolved Mystery of Bigfoot* (First Facts: Unexplained Mysteries). N. Mankato, Minn.: Capstone, 2013.
Find out more facts about the Bigfoot legend in this book.

Townsend, John. *Bigfoot and Other Mysteries* (Crabtree Contact). New York: Crabtree, 2009.
You will find out more about Bigfoot and other mysteries in this book.

Worth, Bonnie. *Looking for Bigfoot* (Step into Reading: Level 4). New York: Random House, 2010.
This book tells the tale of a Bigfoot sighting.

Web sites

Facthound offers a safe, fun way to find Internet sites related to this book. All of the sites on Facthound have been researched by our staff.

Here's all you do:
Visit *www.facthound.com*
Type in this code: 9781410979612

Index